ID0409109

the
Boy who Cried
Abba

the
Boy who Cried
Abba

A
PARABLE OF TRUST
AND ACCEPTANCE

—

BRENNAN MANNING

HarperSanFrancisco
An Imprint of HarperCollins*Publishers*

THE BOY WHO CRIED ABBA: *A Parable of Trust and Acceptance.*
Copyright © 1997 by Brennan Manning. All rights reserved. Printed
in the United States of America. No part of this book may be used or
reproduced in any manner whatsoever without written permission
except in the case of brief quotations embodied in critical articles
and reviews. For information address HarperCollins Publishers, 10
East 53rd Street, New York, NY 10022.

HarperCollins Web Site: http://www.harpercollins.com

HarperCollins®, 📖®, and HarperSanFrancisco™ are trademarks
of HarperCollins Publishers Inc.

FIRST EDITION

Library of Congress Cataloging-in-Publication Data:

Manning, Brennan.
    The boy who cried abba : a parable of trust and acceptance /
Brennan Manning. —1st ed.
        p. cm.
    ISBN 0–06–065456–2 (cloth)
    I. Title.
PS3563.A5365B6   1997
813'.54—dc21   97–3715

97 98 99 00 01 ❖ RRD(H) 10 9 8 7 6 5 4 3 2 1

Abba, you stretch wide your loving arms to me
in the darkest, loneliest moment in my life.

Foreword

I WAS ONE OF MANY LISTENERS WHO FIRST HEARD Brennan speak from a music festival stage just outside of Boston several summers ago. He spoke of his conversion experience in a way I had never considered before.

Brennan's response to the love of God was so honest. He came up from his knees and ran outside under the stars, shaking his fist and screaming up toward heaven: "You are crazy . . . crazy to love me like that!" Brennan's passion, disbelief, amazement, confusion, joy, and gratefulness for the love of God and His gift of salvation released us all to experience again the wonder of being loved ourselves.

What a gift Brennan has given each of us, rekindling our own wonderment at the greatest gift of all.

AMY GRANT

As WILLIE JUAN MADE HIS WAY THROUGH THE VIL-
lage, he was filled with anticipation. Today was the
Fiesta of the Virgin of the Assumption, an occasion
of great celebration in every town along the Rio
Grande. The village of Hopi may have been only a
poor, rough-edged village clinging for survival to
the banks of a very muddy river, but the people of
Hopi loved their festivals. When the once prosper-
ous silver- and lead-mining operations depleted the
ore and pulled out seventy or so years ago, many
people moved away. Now the village survived thanks
only to a few goats, a handful of sheep, and the vari-
ous vegetables that were farmed on the few surrounding fields.

Willie Juan maneuvered through the village of small adobe huts, heading toward the outskirts of town. As he looked up, he could see the sharp peaks of the Sierra Padre rising in the west. The brilliant whites and pinks and yellows of the adobe stood out in contrast to the deeply shadowed granite of the mountains and the cloudless blue summer sky. The August sun made the colors shimmer and dance, almost as if anticipating the joy of the fiesta.

Hopi was a weary village, its buildings bending under the pressures of time and the elements. Most of its adobe huts had but a single light bulb powered by a rooftop solar panel hooked up to a car battery. The older adobe buildings crumbled and melted away under the assault of wind and rain. Heaps of rocks on the surrounding hillsides masked the abandoned mines that once supported the community. Scrubby desert plants like *ocatillo* and prickly pear grew in spite of the harsh, dry conditions. The summer heat was brutal, over 100 degrees today.

Willie Juan didn't notice the heat as he moved quickly through the village. He secretly hoped today would be different, but he'd learned early in life that he didn't really fit in, that he wasn't like the other boys and girls. Even in his own village he'd discovered that people, even kids, can be cruel to those who are different. At school, the kids laughed at his odd skin color, tugged at his burnt-orange hair, and sometimes kicked his stiff leg.

Willie Juan reached the center of the village and quickly joined in the fun at the fiesta. His spirits were high; his eyes sparkled. The fiesta was one of the highlights of the summer, and everyone in the village took time off work to celebrate the holiday.

Willie Juan bought himself a spicy hot tamale and eagerly ran off to join the games. He found a group of big kids picking teams for the game of tug-of-war. The thick rope stretched over a large puddle of water that the men of the village had made for the game using buckets and buckets of water. Willie Juan halted in front of the kids, begging to be picked. One boy shrugged and said okay and put Willie Juan at the front of the line. But when the pulling started, his teammates suddenly let go, jerking Willie Juan forward and dragging him through the slimy pool of mud. The kids laughed and laughed at their joke as Willie Juan lifted himself out of the mud and tried to wipe himself clean.

Willie Juan walked away by himself, away from the laughing. He didn't cry. The boys were just joking, he told himself. But it wasn't fun to always be the brunt of the joke.

He decided to watch the parade instead, and then wander around looking at the booths, seeing many beautiful things for sale and smelling the glorious foods from the vendors' carts.

Later, he found his schoolmates pairing up for the wheelbarrow race. This was an exciting race that all the boys loved. They got to show off their strength and speed and make a plaything out of a work tool. The goal of this race was to get across the finish line first with one boy pushing the wheelbarrow while his partner rode inside. Willie Juan hung back, watching quietly, as the Padre organized nine pairs of boys along the starting line, each pair with a wooden wheelbarrow. At the end was a wheelbarrow with only one boy, Tino, left without a partner. The Padre looked up to see Willie Juan standing off to the side by himself and, gesturing wildly, called Willie Juan over to be Tino's partner. Willie Juan let the Padre hustle him into the wheelbarrow, but when he looked up over his shoulder, he could see the anger in Tino's face. Tino did not want Willie Juan for a partner. Willie Juan grabbed the sides of his wheelbarrow and hung on tight as the race began with shrieks and laughter. But halfway to the finish line, his partner Tino veered off the racecourse and dumped Willie Juan into a pile of brambles filled with sharp thorns. The boys laughed at Tino's joke as Willie Juan picked his way out of the brambles and plucked out the thorns. The joke was on him again, but he didn't laugh this time. He left the boys and went back to watch the jugglers and buy a lemonade.

That night Willie Juan limped home to his grandmother, who lived in a tiny house on the outskirts of the village. In her youth, his grand-mother had lived a very different life. She explained to Willie Juan that she'd looked for love in the wrong arms and happiness in the wrong places. But then a great change had come upon her. She gave up her wild ways, changed her name to Calm Sunset, and retreated to live like a recluse in her tiny adobe hut. Visitors were always welcome there, and even though she was very poor she was always generous with her guests—offering a bite to eat, something to drink, and a few words to soothe the soul. This night, after plucking out the stray thorns, she helped Willie Juan bathe off the mud and rubbed his scratched and aching body with a soothing aloe oil.

"Grandmother," he sighed, "why are the other kids so mean to me? Why do I look so funny?"

Calm Sunset tugged up him onto her soft lap and cradled him gently, telling him, as she had many times before, the now familiar story of his birth and the first few years of his life.

"It was a fine day in the village when you were born, Willie Juan. Everyone was curious about you because you are a very unusual boy. Your great-grandfather Jack had come to this country on a boat from Ireland and your great-grandmother Lizzie was a former African slave. That meant your Grandpa John was African-Celtic, and he married your grandmother Mai, who was from Cambodia. So your father, Johnny, was a mixture of Ireland, Africa, and Asia, and he married your mother, Consuela, who was from Mexico. Your mother was my daughter and our ancestors include both Spanish and Indian blood.

"As a result of your very mixed ancestry, you have a very unusual skin color. Your parents called you Willie Juan. When you were still a toddler, you and your parents were involved in a very serious automobile accident. Your right leg was crushed and the burning debris from the accident fell on your face and body, leaving burns all over your black, white, red, and gold skin. The doctors did what they could for your leg and eventually your burns healed, but there were many scars mottling your finely burnished skin. Your hair it didn't touch—it has always been the same bright copper color."

Calm Sunset gently rocked him, stroking his head, ruffling his hair.

"Your father was a farm worker—he picked fruits and vegetables, following the sun and the seasons, traveling around the country from field to field, picking the harvests as they matured. His job meant he was gone for long periods of time. Your mother stayed here to care for you. She herself took a job working in the fields of a local vegetable farm, planting, weeding, harvesting. Your father sent money and letters every week from those strange, far-off places—Florida, Georgia, New Jersey, and Maine—and your mother would read them to you again and again. You loved your father very much and loved to listen to your mother read.

"Then, the letters stopped coming. For many weeks the whole village held its breath along with your mother. We all felt that something must be very wrong. Finally, one afternoon a worker who had traveled with your father returned home. He was very tired, but he made his way to your house to speak to your mother. He had news about your father, he said sadly. He said your father had taken up with another woman, one with more money and a nice house. He would not be coming back to Hopi and we should not expect to hear from him again.

"Your mother was filled with grief and sadness. I can't remember that she ever smiled again after that. And she was desperately short of money to care for you. She increased the hours she worked in the scorching heat of the vegetable fields. After many weeks of sixteen-hour days, she collapsed in the field one afternoon from heat sickness. The first person who ran to her discovered that she was dead. After that I brought you here to live with me.

"My sweet Willie Juan, the way you were treated today is not a new thing. Widows and orphans are always defenseless. People often think that because you have no parents, that they can be mean to you because no one will step forward to protect you. As much as I love you, I am an old woman and I'm not enough. I'm a poor substitute for the comfort and safety only a living mother and father can provide."

It was true that Calm Sunset lavished the warmth and tenderness of a mother's love on the boy. But she was growing old and feeble, and she could not protect Willie Juan when he was away from her on the streets. Her love and care gave him a safe place to return to at the end of the day, but it was no buffer against the cruelties of a hostile world. And even she could not take away the wounds of the thorns that cruelly pricked Willie Juan deep in his heart.

That night, Willie Juan fell asleep weeping softly in his grandmother's arms. As his tears gave way to sighs, she caressed him tenderly and told him once again, as she had so many times before, about the great El Shaddai and His love for His people, especially the little children. Whenever children saw Him, they flocked to Him and never wanted to leave His side. Long after Willie Juan had drifted to sleep, she continued to rock him and whisper to him of El Shaddai's power and His encompassing care and His tender discipline.

THE DAY AFTER THE FIESTA, WILLIE JUAN WOKE UP sadder than ever. He was so unhappy about having no friends that all he wanted to do was hide. As he left his grandmother's house, he thought of the places he could go to be alone. Then he remembered the cool darkness of the adobe church in the center of the village, with its sweet fragrance of incense and mysterious peace. He'd always been fascinated by the colors and the images and the majestic music. But most of all he was drawn to the big crucifix over the main altar. This day he decided to get a really close look.

Willie Juan entered the quiet church and walked slowly down the side aisle. Pleased that the sacred place was empty, he struggled to pull a stepladder from the sacristy over to the main altar and then climbed up to inspect the face of the Man on the Cross. Willie Juan gently touched His face, tracing the brow, the cheeks, the chin. Then Willie Juan looked up into His eyes. His eyes were so sad, so gentle, so kind. As Willie Juan stared, he realized with a start that this was the great El Shaddai, the One who was a friend to all children. Willie Juan continued to caress the face, recalling his grand-mother's quiet words about this loving Man, allow-ing the truth of his discovery to wash over him again and again, until he understood to the very center of his being that this was the One Who loved him.

The Man looked thirsty, and Willie Juan felt sorry for him. He scrambled down off the steplad-der, got a cup of water, and scrambled back up, try-ing not to spill it. Carefully, he poured the cool water into the half-open mouth of the Man on the Cross. But the statue did not move its lips, and the water ran down the painted chin and splashed onto the altar below. A few drops splashed onto the painted cheeks, making it look like the sad eyes had let fall some tears.

Suddenly Willie Juan heard scornful laughter. He twisted around quickly, nearly losing his balance, and saw three of his classmates who had sneaked in through the side door of the church and had watched Willie Juan try to comfort the Man on the Cross. After jeering at him they ran over to the parish house and told the priest, who came running back with them.

"*Never, never, never* tamper with holy things!" the priest scolded Willie Juan.

"But, but, Padre, he looked so thirsty, and I just wanted to help him. . . ." Willie Juan tried to explain about the Man's sad, gentle, piercing eyes as he quickly scrambled down off the stepladder and tugged it back to the sacristy.

The priest only scoffed at him. "They're just paint!" he huffed. "Why are you trying to pour water down the throat of a wooden statue? You'll just ruin it! Besides, we live in an age of resurrection-centered theology." He told Willie Juan about the *parousia,* and about ascensions and assumptions, and about eschatological realities, and all of the other wonderful things he had learned in his seminary training (or he himself had learned from his own reading).

Willie Juan listened politely and said "Thank you" as he backed out the door of the church. He walked down by the edge of the river, thinking about the wet tears on the painted face. Willie Juan quickly forgot everything the priest told him, but he did not forget the Man with the sad, gentle, and beautiful eyes.

THE SUMMER ENDED AND THE COOLING DAYS OF autumn blew in over the mountains. Time passed by quickly as Willie Juan started back to school. As the weeks went by, Willie Juan's thoughts returned again and again to the Man on the Cross. And when he recalled His eyes, Willie Juan was filled with a myriad of emotions, from compassion to curiosity to wonder.

He was also looking forward to the Fiesta of the Virgin of Guadalupe, which was the next big celebration in their village. Held in mid-December, the fiesta was a rollicking, joyful celebration. There were fireworks, dancing, a costumed religious pageant, a jalapeña festival, and a torchlight procession that wound through the entire village. Best of all, there was a special carnival just for the children.

He had been saving up money from his job caring for the village donkey. Although it was a job that no one else wanted, to Willie Juan it was an important job: the village had one burro, called Pedro, who lived in the center of town. Because the village had no generator to pump water, it was necessary to travel out to the *arriba*—the well in the desert—to carry back a family's ration of water. Until four years ago, there had been running water, pushed to the huts by an electric pump running off the only generator in the village. Then one black night a howling thunderstorm silenced the generator, and the water flowed no more.

After school, Willie Juan and Pedro would make the trip many times, bringing back loads of water for those who needed it. Willie Juan then fed the animal and gave him clean straw to lie down on. For this Willie Juan earned fourteen *pesetas* a week.

By the time the great day of the fiesta arrived, Willie Juan had saved up seventy-eight *pesetas*. With an additional twenty-two that Calm Sunset had given him, he set out for the fair clutching one hundred *pesetas* to spend on anything he liked. As he limped eagerly into the village square his eyes danced as he saw the prancing ponies of the carousel, the cotton-candy stand, the ladies in their brilliantly colored swirling skirts, the men in their sequined *sombreros* worn just once a year, and the colorful clown in a zebra suit dancing like a gazelle.

The air was filled with music and laughter and the mouth-watering smells of cooking food. There were old favorites like fajitas, burritos, hot tortillas, chili tacos, chilis rellenos, and nachos, and the special fiesta foods of enchiladas stuffed with chicken, pork stew with chilis and black beans, frijoles rancheros, green chili stew, savory corn bread, Raggedy Ann pudding, and sweet potato pie. Vendor after vendor lined the square, fires dancing merrily beneath the skillets, fragrant steam bellowing into the air.

Willie Juan was wandering around, absorbing the fiesta, trying to decide whether he should buy a simple tortilla or a plump, juicy fajita, when he caught sight of an old wooden wagon hitched to a small sorrel mare. On the side of the wagon hung a sign, "The Great Medicine Show." Curious, he headed over toward the wagon, pausing at the edge of the crowd. Suddenly he felt his heart rise in his throat. A tall, gaunt, angular Man had stepped out of the buckboard and was about to speak when he stared across the crowd of people straight at Willie Juan. The Man's face was as worn and weather-beaten as the wagon wheels. But the eyes, the eyes . . .

Oh, Madre, it is El Shaddai, Willie Juan breathed. He knew right away, because the eyes were so sad, so gentle, so piercing, and so kind. And then the Man smiled at Willie Juan, his face glowing like a sunburst over the Sierra Padre, his eyes sparkling with joy.

"Hello, Little Brother," he beamed. "I have been waiting for you. I hoped I would see you today."

Willie Juan was startled. He was not used to this sort of greeting. People were not usually pleased to see him.

"Come here and stand by me," the man said, placing his scarred hand on Willie Juan's copper hair with a gentle tousle. "Tell me your name."

"My name is Willie Juan," said the boy, ducking his head and shrugging.

Pulling him closer, the Man gently tilted Willie Juan's face up to his. "People call me Medicine Man."

The Man smiled. "You seem very alone, Willie Juan." He turned and reached into the back of his wagon.

"I have a special gift for you, Little Brother," he said, handing Willie Juan a small bottle containing a clear orange ointment. "Rub three drops on your heart—one tonight, one tomorrow, and one the next day—and wonderful things will happen."

Willie Juan reached into his pocket for *pesetas*, but the Medicine Man stopped him, saying, "Keep your money, Willie Juan. What I have freely received, I freely give."

A small crowd gathered, but no one reached for this potion, which the Medicine Man explained was called "amorine," or Medicine of Love. It had, he claimed, miraculous healing powers—especially for heart trouble.

"Ha! All I'd get from that phony stuff," one man shouted, "is a good case of heartburn."

The crowd laughed in delight.

"That's true," the Medicine Man answered softly. "Your heart would burn." But no one heard him except Willie Juan.

The crowd continued to laugh and mock good-naturedly, slowly drifting away. No one took a single bottle, even though the Medicine Man was willing to give it away. All alone now, he sat down in the buckboard.

Willie Juan approached him and asked in a shy voice, "Señor, will the ama—amor—uh, the stuff in this bottle, will it make my crooked leg straight and make my scars go away?" Willie Juan was startled by what happened next. The Medicine Man picked him up and sat him on his knee. Willie Juan was frightened. He was afraid that when the Medicine Man saw his skin up close, with all the scars, he'd start to laugh, like all the people in the village who had nicknamed him "Speckled Trout."

But the Medicine Man did not laugh. Instead, he drew Willie Juan in close, resting the burnt-orange head next to his heart. It was so warm and peaceful there that Willie Juan thought of the fireplace in the hut where he and his grandmother lived. But then he felt drops of water on his head, and he looked up to see tears streaming from the Medicine Man's eyes. He thought at first that the Medicine Man was hurt, but then realized as he looked into the loving eyes that these were tears of compassion. He thought of his mother. He had felt love in the arms of his mother and grandmother before, but never love like this.

Willie Juan snuggled back against the Medicine Man's heart, clutched the bottle of amorine in his hand, and waited patiently for the answer.

"Willie Juan, my medicine is so powerful that not only will it straighten your crooked leg, it will straighten all winding paths, and all crooked hearts. Through my amorine, every valley of pain shall be filled; every mountain of pride shall be leveled; and all humankind shall see the salvation of El Shaddai."

Willie Juan really didn't understand that. But he did understand when the Medicine Man asked, "Little Brother, would you like to share some lunch with me?" Willie Juan couldn't believe it—sharing a meal was a sign of friendship, and in his whole life no one had ever invited Willie Juan to share a meal. In fact, no one in his whole life—except his mother and Calm Sunset—had ever asked him to share anything. Feelings Willie Juan never even knew existed welled up in his heart. In his own village, Willie Juan was an outsider, isolated and unwanted. But the Medicine Man wanted to share his own lunch pail with him!

Willie Juan was beside himself with joy. He reached into his pocket, pulled out all his *pesetas*, and exclaimed, "I'll buy dessert—cotton candy, lemon ices, dandelion cookies—anything you want!"

They ate heartily; never was a meal so sweet. Willie Juan talked excitedly; the Medicine Man listened quietly. Willie Juan spoke about the death of his father and mother, the accident, his grandmother and her healing aloe oil, how hard school was, and how he wished that he had a friend. He looked up into the Medicine Man's sad, gentle eyes and grew bold enough to ask, "Señor . . . Señor . . . would you be my friend?"

"Willie Juan, I *am* your friend," the Medicine Man quietly answered.

"Yippee!! I'm so happy," Willie Juan clapped gleefully. "I can't wait to tell my grandmother. As soon as I get home I'm going to tell her that I have a new friend. She will be happy, too."

They finished eating and began to clean up. As they gathered up the leftovers, Willie Juan noticed that the Medicine Man's lunch pail wasn't large enough to contain all the fragments. Willie Juan found a grocery bag to help carry the leftovers home. Calm Sunset could enjoy sharing the meal as well.

Then without warning, a cold chill gripped Willie Juan's heart. *I never had a friend before,* he realized. *And I don't know how friends act. The Medicine Man is so kind to me: he shares his food, he doesn't laugh at my scarred skin, he listens to me. What if I am not a good friend? What if I disappoint him? What if he changes his mind? I could lose my only friend!*

Panic shook the whole of his little frame, and Willie Juan grabbed the Medicine Man's hand and cried out, "Oh, Señor, please tell me, what does it mean to be a friend?"

"Don't let your heart be troubled, Little Brother," replied the Medicine Man. "I'll share with you what friendship means to me—and by the way, it means a great deal. I consider it life's rarest and most price-less treasure. I'll tell you the kind of friend I am, and then you decide for yourself, Willie Juan, what kind of friend you want to be."

"Yes, Señor."

"Little Brother, if I speak to you in any language, human or angelic—but do not love you, I am not your friend. If I share all my knowledge with you so that you understand everything in the whole wide world—but do not love you, I am no friend at all. If I give all my food to feed your family and give all my money to take care of all your needs—but do not love you, I am not your friend. Willie Juan, because I am your friend, I will always be patient with you. I will always be kind to you. I will never be jealous of your other friends. I will never act stuck-up with you. I will never be rude to you. I won't befriend you just to get what I can from you. I won't lose my temper when you disappoint me. Nor will I rejoice when you do wrong things, but I *will* celebrate when you are true to yourself. There will be no limit to my forgiveness of your failings, to my trust in you, to my power to endure all the difficulties of being your friend. Willie Juan, I will never fail you."

The little boy, entranced by the Medicine Man's words, grew quiet and snuggled closer.

"Little Brother?"

Willie Juan startled. "Uh, yes, Señor?"

"Are you going to remember everything I've been telling you?"

"Oh no, Señor—I mean, yes—I mean, uh . . . " Willie Juan was confused.

"If you have forgotten everything I have just said," the Medicine Man responded, "just remember this. There are three things that matter in a friendship: faith and hope in your friend, but the third is the greatest of them all, the love of your friend."

Willie Juan had listened attentively, but he knew that he had much to learn about being a friend. He shook his head sadly. "Oh Señor, that is so beautiful, but I could never be a friend like that! I'm just a little boy. And I've never had a friend. I'm sure I'll just mess up."

"That's why I gave you my amorine, Little Brother. It will help you learn what you need to know to be a friend. You will need to rub the three drops on your heart—one tonight, one tomorrow, and one the third day. The first drop is called Forgiveness of Others; the second is called Acceptance of Self; and the third is called Joy. Do that, and you'll have done your part. The Spirit of El Shaddai will do the rest."

"Is that when it will heal my leg and my scars?"

"Yes, my little friend, when the Spirit of El Shaddai comes upon you, then you will be healed. But tonight after you rub on the first drop, accept in faith, never doubting. If you doubt you will be like a wave tossed and driven by the wind or a tumbleweed hurtling across the sand without roots. People like that, who are slippery in all they do, must not expect to receive anything from the Spirit of El Shaddai. But you, Willie Juan—ask and you will receive; seek and you will find; knock, and the door will open to you."

He paused. "And now, Willie Juan, I must leave. I say good-bye because I am going home to my father."

"What—what?" gasped Willie Juan. "Can I come with you?"

The sudden announcement left him feeling abandoned, lonely, and afraid. In a pleading voice he cried, "Señor, can I come with you?"

"No, where I'm going you can't come, Willie Juan. It's a long journey. I must cross over the

Sandias Mountains, go down through the sands of the Arizona desert, then across the wilderness of the Rockies, through the dense redwood forests, and then over the great sea to the kingdom of my father. But, in my father's kingdom, there are many beautiful houses. I'm going to fix up a place especially for you. Then I'm going to come back and take you home with me, so that we can be together."

"Señor, who is your father?"

"I call him Abba."

Willie Juan began to giggle. "Abba, Abba, Abba . . . ." He let it roll around in his mouth, feeling how easy it was to say, how funny it sounded. It made his lips tingle when he said it quickly. Then he grew suddenly quiet. He was sorry he'd laughed. The Medicine Man had just told him that a friend was never rude. Maybe he wouldn't like people to laugh at his father's name.

"I'm sorry, Señor," Willie Juan said. "I didn't mean to make fun of your father's name. Please don't be angry that I laughed about his name."

"No, Little Brother," the Medicine Man responded. "My father's always pleased when you call his name, even when you play with it." At the mere mention of his father's name, the Medicine Man's face shone like a thousand sunbeams, and his eyes grew brilliant like starlight.

The Medicine Man lifted Willie Juan off his lap and helped him stand up. Willie Juan stood quietly and watched as the Man began to pack up his buckboard and prepare to leave on his journey.

"Don't forget tonight, Little Brother. And by the way, thank you for the cup of water you gave me in the adobe church. I will not forget it. It will not go unrewarded." The Medicine Man smiled one more smile, blessing Willie Juan with his peace. He climbed into the buckboard and with a soft cluck to his horse, he headed west, away from the fiesta and the little town of Hopi.

Willie Juan ran, skipped, jumped, and danced all the way home. He sang, too, even though his third-grade teacher, Sister Mary Picayune, had told him that he must never, never sing in church because his voice sounded like something called the Abomination of Desolation—whatever that meant. He sang anyway, remembering a tune from the folk service: "Oh, he called the little children, and sat 'em on his knee; glory, sing to the Lord. Then he hugged 'em and caressed 'em, till they didn't want to leave him; glory, sing to the Lord."

THAT NIGHT, WILLIE JUAN EXCITEDLY TOLD HIS grandmother about the fiesta: the parades and the lively music and the delicious foods. And he told her that he had found a new friend, although he didn't say much about this friend. Calm Sunset could see that Willie Juan had indeed had a very exciting day. He was filled with energy, unable to sit still, obviously filled with the joy of finding such a wonderful new friend.

Willie Juan quickly ate his supper, then kissed his grandmother good night, and went to his own little corner of the adobe hut, drawing the curtain across. He was eager to try the Medicine of Love. Wouldn't Grandmother be surprised when all his scars had disappeared and his leg was straight and whole! He knelt down beside his bed and pulled out the little orange bottle. He opened it slowly, then tipped it carefully to place a small drop on his finger. He began to rub the first drop of amorine, Forgiveness of Others, onto his heart.

"Ow, that hurts!" he exclaimed in surprise as he felt the amorine begin to burn inside his chest. Willie Juan hadn't realized how deeply the other boys and girls had hurt him. But he continued to rub it in anyway, because that's what the Medicine Man had told him to do. As he rubbed, he recalled the pain of being rejected, the humiliation of being ridiculed, the sorrow of being abandoned. The tears slowly welled and fell as Willie Juan cautiously began to forgive. His father . . . his schoolmates . . . the villagers . . . even his mother. At first the pain of forgiving nearly overwhelmed him, because the memories of abandonment and rejection were so vivid, the hurt still so real, and the pain still so deep. But gradually, as he let go, Willie Juan began to feel the hurt recede and peace flood into his heart.

He was so eager for healing that he decided not to wait another day before applying the next drop. He started to open the bottle so he could pour out the second drop, Acceptance of Self.

Then, in the moonlight streaming through the window, Willie Juan looked down and caught sight of his scarred, disfigured torso. He moaned. The hideous scars glowed with a dappled iridescence that made the boy shudder in disgust. He became furious. "I hate you, Speckled Trout!" he screamed at himself. "You stink! You're just a big mistake! You're uglier than a lizard! Ugly, stupid, rotten! I hate you, I hate you!" He threw himself across his bed and curled up into a little ball, flinging the bottle away.

Even worse than seeing his own scarred body was the anguish of betrayal. The Medicine Man had tricked him. Willie Juan's leg was not straight, his scars had not disappeared, his body was still broken and marred. The Medicine Man made promises he didn't keep.

"I should never have trusted you, you stupid Medicine Man! You're a faker, you're a phony, you're more bent than a broken nose! You lied to me!" he cried. "I hate you!"

Feeling deceived, abandoned, and friendless once more, Willie Juan began to cry with such desperation that his whole body shook with the quiet sobbing. Finally, physically spent and emotionally exhausted, he sank into a troubled sleep.

The next morning Willie Juan shuffled into the kitchen. Calm Sunset sat rocking gently in her chair. She watched Willie Juan tenderly and wondered at his puffy eyes and sad face. She wondered that she hadn't heard his weeping during the night. What happened to turn last night's elation into this morning's sadness?

"Come and sit by my side, precious child," she murmured. The boy nestled into the rocker beside his grandmother. "Tell me what is going on in your sad little life."

Like a swollen river rolling over the levee, the words gushed in a torrent of pain from Willie Juan's mouth. The encounter with the Medicine Man at the fiesta, seeing the gentle eyes of El Shaddai, having a friend for the first time, his new name for God, Abba, the bottle of amorine, and last night's heart-wrenching failure with the drop called Self-Acceptance.

With her eyes closed, Calm Sunset sat motionless for a long time. She had listened intently to her grandson's story. Now she was listening even more intently to an inner voice. Then she placed her arm around Willie Juan's shoulders and said, "You are light to my fading eyes, Little One, and the love of my weary heart. How much do I love you? There is no way I can ever tell you how much. Let me ask you something. Do you know why the Medicine Man, when he was standing in front of the buckboard at the fiesta looking out at the whole crowd, do you know why he fixed his gaze on you?"

"No, Grandmother."

"It was because when he saw you, he saw himself, Willie Juan—wounded, outcast, lonely, and betrayed. In a single instant, he understood you and read the longing in your eyes. Ah, my little child, I must tell you with a heavy heart that so many who claim to know El Shaddai do not long for Him—even though they crisscross the globe speaking as if they were on intimate terms with Him. Everyone who meets these people assumes that they must be close to Him—but in truth, many of them are simply afraid to be alone with the Medicine Man. They're frightened of becoming still enough to rest in His presence. They flee silence; they dread solitude. Oh, they always use all the right words—getting honest, becoming open, being vulnerable. And yet they remain dishonest, closed, and invulnerable to the Lover in our midst. Someday, tragedy and heartbreak may force them to turn their own words upon themselves, but now their hearts are empty of the fierce longing that consumes yours, Willie Juan."

Relaxed in his grandmother's arms and soothed by her quiet words, Willie Juan was yawning, tired from his long, restless night. His grandmother didn't notice.

"Let me explain the second drop of amorine. You can't get self-acceptance by memorizing Scripture or by trying hard to make people like you or by working hard to achieve great things. It is a work of El Shaddai, the all-powerful One. It is an act of trust, the triumph of grace over illusion, the victory of truth over self-delusion. . . . "

Calm Sunset glanced down. Willie Juan was sound asleep, curled up at her side. His grand-mother smiled. Then she started chuckling—mostly at herself. *Ah, you silly old woman. You are as sensitive as a red brick! You bored the child to sleep with your endless pontificating! Perhaps you are not so wise after all. O Lord, have mercy on this addle-brained old woman.*

She leaned back in the rocking chair, closed her eyes, and turned her face to the morning sun, quietly stroking Willie Juan's copper hair. As she rocked, she heard a soft sound very much like a bubbling brook. She knew it was Jesus laughing with her.

When he awoke a few hours later, Calm Sunset fixed a breakfast of hot tortillas and beans for her grandson. During the meal, Calm Sunset realized what must happen next.

"Willie Juan, listen carefully to me now," she said with quiet urgency. "You must leave here immediately and go to the Cave of Bright Darkness."

The boy's eyes grew wide. "Grandmother, why must I go there? Will you come with me?"

"I am too old to make the trip, Little One. And besides, this is a trip you can take only by yourself. When you reach the cave, you must stay there until one hour after sunset. Sit calmly and patiently. Listen to the silence. Watch for water, wind, and fire, and then wait for the storm to pass. It is not important that you understand what I am saying. At this moment, courage is more important than understanding."

Calm Sunset helped Willie Juan pack a knapsack with a plump fajita left over from his lunch with the Medicine Man, a canteen of water, and a flashlight. At the last minute, she remembered the amorine. "Quick, Little One, run and find your bottle of the Medicine of Love." Willie Juan ran to the corner and dug around behind his bed to find the little bottle he'd flung away the night before. They tucked it into the backpack and Calm Sunset helped Willie Juan slip his arms through the straps of the backpack.

"Be on your way, Willie Juan." Her eyes glistened with love, and her voice rang with such authority that Willie Juan did not hesitate. She marked his forehead with the sign of the cross and hugged him tenderly. He departed at once.

With the knapsack strapped across his shoulders, Willie Juan scrambled across the slope that led to the steep ascent up the mountain. The Cave of Bright Darkness had been hollowed out of the face of the mountain by natural erosion and stood at an elevation of five thousand feet. The cave had come by its name through more than three centuries of use by countless pilgrims as a place of spiritual retreat. Those who spoke of their experiences found them difficult to describe, telling of shattering spiritual encounters there in the luminous obscurity of pure faith or, as Calm Sunset had put it after her retreat there some sixty years earlier, in the deep and dazzling darkness of sheer trust.

Willie Juan could never understand what the pilgrims were talking about. He only knew that the Cave of Bright Darkness was a holy place, perhaps as sacred as the church in the village. He knew that it was sacred because those who visited the Cave of Bright Darkness met El Shaddai. And now Willie Juan had become a pilgrim as well.

Hours later, as the sun began its descent behind the far ridges of the Sierra Padre, Willie Juan pulled himself up onto the final rim. Before him a stone staircase wound down from the ridge to end on the ledge in front of the cave. Wearied by the long climb, his stiff leg throbbing with the effort, Willie Juan moved slowly down the seventeen steps, plopping down onto the parapet in front of the cave. He shrugged off his backpack, then reached for his canteen, tilted his head back, and drank deeply. He looked out over the valley, realizing with some surprise that he'd never climbed this high before. His limp generally kept him down on the more gentle slopes near the village, except for one time that now came back to him. Last summer, his classmate

Antonio had dared him to climb to the narrow ridge. Willie Juan took the dare and began climbing. He was doing fine until he placed his good foot on a loose rock that rolled away and caused him to tumble down the slope. The jagged stones tore holes in his pants and made his knees and elbows fiery with pain. His hands were shredded by small cuts and wherever he touched his clothes they had left bloody smears. He remembered how hard it had been to see through his tears, and how Antonio had laughed and mocked him as Willie Juan had looked at him helplessly. "Willie Juan, you wimp! I ain't gonna play with you no more."

As the painful memory passed, Willie Juan got to his feet and entered the cave.

It was cool inside. The massive granite walls stabilized the temperature at sixty degrees, even on the hottest day in summer or the coldest day in winter. The little boy looked around the interior, which was twelve yards wide and six yards deep. A stone slab about halfway back into the cave served as a bed, with a few burlap bags that served as a mattress as well as blankets. In one corner there was a kerosene lamp, a rickety chair, and a battered oak table. An alcove in the other corner served as a tiny chapel. It had a stone altar and a tiny tabernacle made out of wrought iron interlaced with red velvet fabric. A tall crucifix stood behind the altar. Other than that, the cave was bare.

Willie Juan limped toward the stone slab, clambered up on top, and wrapped two burlap sacks around himself. The strenuous climb had sapped all his strength. Within minutes, he was sound asleep.

An hour later, the little boy was startled awake by a deafening noise that sounded like the sharp report of a rifle. In fact, it was a teeth-rattling peal of thunder accompanied by a howling wind and a relentless rain that slashed across the sky. Fascinated, Willie Juan slipped off the slab and stepped into the mouth of the cave. Suddenly, a fierce bolt of lightning struck the shrubs and the wildflowers a hundred yards below, setting them ablaze. The wild fury of the hurricane-force storm crashed against the mountainside in unabated intensity. Wide-eyed with wonder, Willie Juan stared into the maelstrom. He was so transfixed by the cosmic spectacle that he was utterly unaware that he was unafraid.

Then, as if by a stern command from the Master of the wind and the waves, the storm abruptly ceased. Silence slowly blanketed the Sierra Padre. So palpable was the quiet that the little boy felt himself becoming as silent as the valley before him, entering an interior place he had never visited before: total inward stillness.

Out of the stillness came the whisper of a Voice: "Willie Juan."

Too startled to answer, Willie Juan looked around to see who was speaking.

"Willie Juan," came the whisper once again.

"Y-yes? I'm here. I'm Willie Juan. Who are you?"

"To most I am known as Danger, Willie Juan. I make my presence known in water, wind, and fire. I am Spirit, without shape, form, or face. Those who seek safety try to summon me like a tame lapdog. They crave security instead of growth. They have no tolerance for mystery, certain that they can know everything knowable. The weak-kneed do not love Danger. They are afraid I will call them to become what they are not. They call me Comforter for all the wrong reasons and are surprised when no comfort comes to them."

Willie Juan sat very still and listened carefully, tilting his head as if to hear better.

"You're a brave boy, Willie Juan," the Voice continued. "You have made a frightening journey alone to this secluded mountaintop. None of the other boys has done that. You are braver than Antonio, who mocked you as tumbled down the trail; braver than Tino, who dumped you into the brambles; more courageous than your weathervane friends who let go of the rope in the tug-of-war game. Your journey has begun in promise, Little Friend, but it could end in failure unless you are brave enough to risk the next step.

"You see, Willie Juan, the Evil One, like a shrewd enemy commander, has surrounded you and discovered where you are most vulnerable. He has used your bad feelings about your scars and lame leg to tie you up in knots, chaining you to a deep sense of worthlessness. The next step can be dangerous, because you will need to let go of your hold on your life. You'll feel as if you're losing control, and the illusion of being in charge of your own future, of being the master of your own destiny, will vanish. For the first time in your life, you will understand just how needy and dependent you really are. It's risky, without doubt—but it will set you on the road to freedom. Do you have the courage, Little One?"

"Um, uh, what is this next step?" Willie Juan asked timidly, clasping his hands tightly.

"Surrender yourself in unwavering trust to El Shaddai. Trust that everything that has happened to you was necessary to bring you to this present moment. And trust that the good work that has been started within you will be brought to completion. Are you open to receive this gift, Little Friend?"

Willie Juan considered his words, thinking, *Danger has just told me that I am braver than all the boys in Hopi. I mustn't disappoint him. I will* not *disappoint him.*

"Oh, please, yes, I want it," he exclaimed. "I want your gift!"

Then the Voice said, "You have the heart of your grandmother Calm Sunset." And with those words the Spirit washed over the little boy with such gentle force that it knocked Willie Juan backwards into the chair, which collapsed into pieces under him. Stunned, Willie Juan rolled off the broken scraps and started to get up when he heard the Voice again.

"Be still, Willie Juan. Lie back on the ground and listen closely. That rickety chair is like your old life of mistrust. It has just splintered into scraps," said the Voice. "Now lie back on the ground. Think about your grandmother, and then make ready for the One whose smile, like lightning, will set free the song of glory that now sleeps inside your soul."

Obedient to the Spirit, Willie Juan lay back on the floor of the cave and remembered sacred times from the past with his grandmother—how proud of him she'd been when he returned from his first day at school . . . How it had pained her when the other boys mistreated him . . . How she would smile when he kissed her on the cheek . . . How she had been kind to him when he grew sad and sulked, forgetting to do his chores around the house . . . How her love never changed despite his funny looks or his sulkiness or what he did. He remembered how Calm Sunset's eyes had glistened with love and confidence as he prepared to leave for the Cave of Bright Darkness. He knew deep down that his grandmother loved him—that his mother and even his father had loved him, once—but in his mind he still could not understand how they could love a Speckled Trout, why they never seemed to notice how ugly he was. Yet in his heart he knew that their love was real.

Suddenly, Willie Juan's remembering was interrupted by the sound of footsteps on the stone stairwell. He looked up quickly. The Medicine Man filled the mouth of the cave.

"Normally, it's my custom to stand at the door and knock," he said with a twinkle in his eye. "But since you don't have a door—may I come in?"

Willie Juan's eyes bulged, his mouth hung open, his heart raced.

"Oh, Padre, it is the Medicine Man!" he gasped, jumping up and running to him. His feelings were all jumbled up inside his chest—the happiness of seeing his friend once again, the painful memories of giving up on the amorine and denouncing the Medicine Man as a fake, fear that the Medicine Man would learn of his angry outburst and realize that Willie Juan had betrayed their friendship.

"It is well that you exclaim 'Padre,' Little Brother. You're wiser than you know: he who sees me sees the Father, sees Abba."

Barely able to breathe, Willie Juan stared at the Medicine Man's smiling face. His face looked more beautiful than a heaven full of stars and a radiant Hopi sunset and the glistening eyes of his grandmother all put together.

"I know my colleague Danger came by earlier,"

said the Medicine Man. "He knows me in a way that no human being can ever know me. He taught you that unconditional trust is the seal of friendship. Trust is not out at the edges of our friendship, but at its heart and center. He knows that in order to be my friend and understand my teaching you must learn to trust me unconditionally. Trust is at the very center of all my friendships.

"He's very powerful, isn't he, Willie Juan? When you pray, 'Come, Holy Spirit, and give me what I want,' you'd better duck. Calling on him can be like going to the dentist to fix your upper left molar and hearing him say after a brief inspection, 'I'm sorry, but I'll have to remove your whole mouth.' When you ask him into your life, he changes it in ways you can't even imagine."

The Medicine Man chuckled but grew serious as he looked into Willie Juan's eyes. "I have come to find out how the drops of amorine are working. Tell me, what's been happening?"

Willie Juan's face turned ashen. He lowered his eyes and wiped the tears from his cheeks. "Yesterday,

I said some very bad things about you, Señor. I
didn't trust you. I called you a faker, a phony. I was
so mad at you I said I hated you—"

"—Hush, hush, Little Friend. I'm used to being
called bad names. At least you didn't call me a
drunkard and a glutton, as some of my old adver-
saries did. Little Brother, you were forgiven before
you asked. Now accept that forgiveness and be at
peace. Don't punish yourself anymore.

"You know, there is an old saying that friends
have to eat a peck of salt together," he went on,
"before they really know one another. They nicknamed my old friend Peter 'Rock,' yet he failed me
in the time of testing. But, Willie Juan, it only made
our friendship stronger. Real love survives betrayal
and deepens trust."

At that moment, forgiven and free, redeemed
from the corrosive power of mistrust, Willie Juan
glowed like a child just given the sun, his joy filling
his eyes and face.

"Um, uh, want to split my fajita with me?" he
offered humbly.

Willie Juan ran over and snatched up his backpack. Digging for the fajita, he plopped down cross-legged on the floor next to the Medicine Man. He split the fajita carefully, handing half to the Medicine Man, who ate with great gusto. In fact, the Medicine Man attacked the food with such single-minded relish, licking his fingers and smacking his lips, that Willie Juan watched in amazement.

Aware of his rapt attention, the Medicine Man smiled and said, "When you get to heaven, Little Friend, your Abba will not ask you how many prayers you said, or how many souls you saved. He'll ask, 'Did you enjoy the fajita?' He wants you to live with passion, in the beauty of the moment, accepting and enjoying his gifts."

Sipping from the canteen, Willie Juan looked into the sad, gentle, beautiful eyes and asked, "I know now you are truly the Medicine Man, the One my grandmother calls El Shaddai. But why didn't you come to the cave with trumpets and angels and a great big show?"

"I didn't want you to frighten you, my friend. If I came displaying all the glory of El Shaddai, you would find it utterly unbearable and, more importantly, you'd be afraid to come close to me. Isn't it difficult to be a friend to someone who has all the answers, who's always totally unafraid, invulnerable, needing nothing and nobody, always in control of every situation? With a person like that you don't feel comfortable or needed.

"Willie Juan, it is the deepest desire of my heart to be known, loved, and wanted as I really am. There are some people who have fashioned me in their own image and refer to me in grand language as the Supreme Being. But they really do not want a supreme being who has been spit upon and ridiculed. They don't want a supreme being who eats with criminals and the outcasts. When they feel that they have been abandoned by El Shaddai, when their lives fill with loneliness, rejection, failure, and depression, when they are deaf to everything but the shriek of their own pain, then their trust in El Shaddai vanishes as quickly as last night's dream. They dismiss me as a loser, saying that my ministry was a failure, that my life made no difference, that I am only a naked, ineffective, executed pretender. They say that trust in El Shaddai is nice for women, children, the senile, and the naive. It's fine for normal times, they insist, for occasional religious ceremonies. But when the chips are down, when they fear they'll lose all their money or when their safety is threatened, they are convinced that nothing is going to happen unless they make it happen. They are fair-weather friends and there are many of them. They don't want the real me, Willie Juan.

"When I got out of the buckboard at the fiesta and searched the faces of the crowd, my eyes fastened on you because I saw the loneliness in your eyes and felt the longing in your heart. I knew then you wanted me, making my eyes dance and my heart skip. You may have thought you just wanted healing for your body, but way down deep I knew you longed for more. You were more pleased that I called you my friend than that I gave you a small bottle of my Medicine of Love. There were others in the crowd who wanted me, but not with a desire that transcends all other desires. Do you understand, my Little Friend? Their hearts are still divided. They value the affection, the attention, and the approval of others more than they value me."

Comforted and able to find his courage once again, Willie Juan reached deep in his backpack for the bottle of amorine. He held it in his outstretched hand and asked, "Señor, would you rub the second drop on my heart?"

"We'll rub it on together, Little Brother," answered the Medicine Man, wrapping his arms around Willie Juan and pulling him close. "But first you must know that long ago I fashioned you from the clay of the earth and the kiss of my mouth. I loved you, Willie Juan, long before you were in your mother's womb. You're one of a kind, Little Friend. You are beautiful because you reflect my beauty in a way the world has never seen before and will never see again.

"Some people in the village think you're a loser. But those who understand me and the words I speak know the secret I carry in my heart: the losers are really the winners.

"Now, don't think anything, don't intend anything, don't promise to do anything special, Willie Juan. Simply accept that you are accepted. Of course you're weak and flawed—but remember, I don't have any friends who aren't! That's not what matters. All that matters is that you have the courage to accept acceptance. Your acceptance is not rooted in physical appearance, intellectual gifts, athletic skills, popularity, fame, or anything else. It is anchored solely in my acceptance."

With the Medicine Man's great gnarled hands covering Willie Juan's small scarred hands, they rubbed the drop on his heart together. In that single instant, shame retreated, fear vanished, and self-hatred fled out of the cave, over the parapet, and splattered five hundred feet below.

Willie Juan sat in a stunned silence, marveling at the wonder of finding the shame and self-hatred that he had lived with for so long suddenly vanished.

Then the Medicine Man placed a finger under Willie Juan's chin and lifted his face gently, searching the boy's face. "Before I leave, Willie Juan, I must ask you one question. Little Brother, do you love me more than these?"

Gazing back into his intent eyes, Willie Juan knew at once the Medicine Man was asking him if he was willing to give up all the gifts he had just received.

"Tell me—do you love me more than these?"

Willie Juan threw his arms around the Medicine Man's neck and hugged him close.

"Señor, El Shaddai, my Friend, please don't leave me and don't ever let me leave you. Do you know what it's like to wake up in the morning and know that you have a friend to laugh with you when you're happy and not laugh at you when you're dumb? Could we just be together, walking side by side as friends and finding joy in being together?

"You said one time that I don't remember so well and I maybe don't. But I do remember the one thing that you said to me that mattered the most: 'I love you, my friend.' Even if you were just kidding me about my leg and my scars, I don't care. I'd be happy to stay just as I am, if only you would stay with me. All I want is you, Señor! All I want is you."

As the drop of amorine entered Willie Juan's heart, it coursed through his whole body and opened his eyes to see how empty life would be without his Friend. That thought so staggered his mind and appalled his heart that from that night on his life would never be the same.

The drop also opened his eyes to see that right at the bottom of his little heart, he had but one burning desire—not for the things the Medicine Man had promised, but for the Medicine Man himself.

Willie Juan clung to the Medicine Man with his head resting on the Medicine Man's shoulder like a lamb in the arms of a loving shepherd—or a child resting in the arms of his father. The little boy's voice grew hoarse with deep affection.

"I've never said this to anybody before—I love you, my Friend. All I want is you, Señor! All I want is you!"

With a sigh that seemed to rise up out of the depths of his heart, the Medicine Man said, "Willie Juan, I will never leave you—never. Every time you pray in the Spirit, 'Abba, I belong to You,' I'll be in your heart praying with you, because that is my prayer. Let that call, 'Abba,' rise often and easily from the depth of your soul."

"Oh, one more thing, Willie Juan," he added. "Before you run down the mountain to your house, go to the back of the cave and sit in the chapel for a brief moment."

The Medicine Man embraced the little boy with great affection, blessed him once more with his peace, and departed as suddenly as he had arrived.

Just as instructed, Willie Juan turned and moved back to the chapel. He walked into the quiet refuge, savoring its peace and gentle embrace. He stood a moment, letting his eyes adjust to the subdued light, and then slid slowly to the floor. He looked up to the altar, lifting his eyes and raising his arms to the crucifix in thanksgiving—and almost collapsed at what he saw. The torso of the Crucified was tattoocd with Willie Juan's hideous scars. The face was streaked with tears. And the withered right leg of the Crucified had torn away from the nail and hung limply in the air.

The little boy collapsed his head down onto his chest and wrapped his arms around his knees, hugging them tightly. He wept freely, softly crying "Abba. Abba. Abba." And as the tears ran down his face onto his shirt, they burned with a strangely pleasurable sensation. Willie Juan shuddered as a deep gladness welled up within him, gathering such warmth and force that it seemed his chest would surely burst. The tears of the Crucified had combined with his own to rub in the third drop of amorine—Joy—on the heart of the boy who cried "Abba."

Willie Juan had no time to feel the sadness of good-bye. He hurriedly picked up his backpack, canteen, and flashlight and began his scramble down the mountain. An hour later, flashlight in hand, he raced home chanting, "Abba, I belong to you," and rushed into the arms of his grandmother.

This time he fell asleep in a deep and peaceful quiet, not in tears.

By the following morning, word had spread through the entire village of Hopi that little Willie Juan had made the dangerous journey to the Cave of Bright Darkness all alone. Hundreds of people gathered in front of his house. The Padre pushed his way through the crowd, entered the house, and confronted Calm Sunset. "Good heavens!" he said. "What happened to Willie Juan's leg and his scars?"

With the gathered wisdom of her eighty-four years she answered, "Padre, to those who understand, no words are necessary. To those who do not understand, no words are possible. When you become like a little child, when you open your heart to El Shaddai without reservation, not only will you find the answer, but you will discover an entirely new set of questions."

After growing up in Brooklyn and serving with the Marines in the Korean War, Brennan Manning stepped off a career path in journalism in a restless search for something more in life. He entered the Franciscan priesthood, earned academic degrees in philosophy and theology, and embarked on a path of ministry that led from campus work to living among the poor in the U.S. and Europe. Along the way he experienced life-changing encounters with the risen Christ—from a chapel in Loretto, Pennsylvania, to a cave in the Zaragoza Desert of Spain—that forever altered and deepened his understanding of who God is and what God wants of us.

Years later, after suffering a precipitate collapse into alcoholism, he shifted direction and began to focus more on writing and speaking. In 1982 he married and left the priesthood. He's written nine books—many of them, like *The Ragamuffin Gospel,* beloved and warmhearted teaching parables—and he speaks and leads retreats on the subject of intimate encounter with Jesus, providing spiritual direction for people of varied ages and backgrounds.

MONOGRAPHS ON
STATISTICS AND APPLIED PROBABILITY

General Editors

D.R. Cox, D.V. Hinkley, D. Rubin and B.W. Silverman

(Full details concerning this series are available from the Publishers.)